Your Environment

Recycling

Jen Green

Franklin Watts
London • Sydney

How to use this book

This series has been developed for group use in the classroom, as well as for students reading on their own. Its differentiated text allows students of mixed reading abilities to enjoy reading and talking about the same topic.

① The main text and ② picture captions give essential information in short, simple sentences. They are set in the © Sassoon font as recommended by the National Literacy Strategy document *Writing in the Early Years*. This font style helps students bridge the gap between their reading and writing skills.

③ Below each picture caption is a subtext that explains the pictures in greater detail, using more complicated sentence structures and vocabulary.

④ Text backgrounds are cream or a soft yellow to reduce the text/background contrast to support students with visual processing difficulties or other special needs.

Rubbish

Refuse trucks pick up rubbish from your home. ①

They take the rubbish to landfill sites.

⬆ **Trucks collect our waste.** ②

In many countries, a refuse truck ③ visits once a week to collect waste. The collectors empty dustbins onto the truck. ④

PAPERBACK EDITION PRINTED 2007

© Aladdin Books Ltd 2004

Designed and produced by
Aladdin Books Ltd
2/3 Fitzroy Mews
London W1T 6DF

First published in 2004
in Great Britain by
Franklin Watts
338 Euston Road
London NW1 3BH

Franklin Watts Australia
Hachette Children's Books
Level 17/207 Kent Street
Sydney NSW 2000

A catalogue record for this book is available from the British Library.
Dewey Classification: 363.72' 82
ISBN 978-0-7496-7532-5

Printed in Malaysia
Editor: Jim Pipe

Educational Consultant:
Jackie Holderness

Recycling Consultant:
Pete Spriggs, Waste Watch

Design:
Flick, Book Design and Graphics

Picture Research:
Brian Hunter Smart

CONTENTS

Introduction

Waste is anything we no longer have use for. When we throw something away, we create waste.

Activities such as cooking or washing also create waste. Yet, we can recycle waste. Recycling means making waste into something new.

This book explains why we should recycle and how we should do it.

⬆ **A canoe made from old glass!**

You might be surprised what rubbish can be turned into. The glass from bottles and jars can be turned into a material called fibreglass. This mix of strong glue and thin strips of glass can be used to make canoes and boats.

⬇ *We can all learn how to recycle.*

This book explains how we can turn our rubbish into useful products. However, recycling is just one way to deal with waste. Remember these three words: Reduce, Reuse, Recycle.

• Try to reduce, or cut down, the amount of waste you produce.

• Reuse items, such as glass and plastic jars or bottles, when you can find a use for them.

• If you cannot reuse something, then recycle it.

Why do we recycle?

Every day, we all throw things away – wrappers, bottles, empty cans and waste paper.

This rubbish creates a lot of waste. It spoils our surroundings and can harm wildlife.

We don't have to throw rubbish away. We can can recycle it. This means using old things to make new things.

▷ **Look how messy litter is!**

Our rubbish is collected every week. We forget about it. But rubbish does not just go away. Someone has to deal with it. If you just put your rubbish into a bath it would fill 100 baths every year!

Sometimes, people leave rubbish lying around. This is called litter. Litter spoils the look of the countryside, as well as towns. When litter piles up, it can also smell terrible. Just sniff your dustbin!

⬆ Waste can harm wildlife.

Shops, hospitals, farms, factories and power stations all produce different kinds of waste. Some of this waste is poisonous and harmful to wildlife. If waste pollutes (dirties) a beach, it can take years to make it clean again.

⬆ More people in the world means more waste.

When there were fewer people, waste did not matter so much. Now, big towns and cities are found in most parts of the world. The large numbers of people living everywhere produce lots of waste.

⬇ Look in your dustbin.

The type of rubbish we throw away has changed over the years. About 70 years ago, most of the waste in the bin was ash and dust from coal fires that were used to heat houses. That is how "dust" bins got their name!

A lot of rubbish today is packaging. Many products are wrapped up or put in boxes. Once we take out the product, we throw away the packaging.

What is recycling?

The rubbish we throw away contains materials we can use again.

At recycling centres, we can separate our rubbish into different materials. Factories can use these materials to make all kinds of new products.

When we recycle, we do not have to bury or burn our waste.

▷ **This is a recycling centre. A woman is bringing her old glass bottles.**

Many recycling centres have a different container for each type of material:

- Glass bottles (green, brown or clear glass)
- Newspapers and magazines
- Textiles (old clothes)
- Cans
- Cardboard
- Plastic bottles and bags

You can prepare cans, bottles and other containers for recycling by washing them out and removing the tops and labels.

Newspaper ——

Plastic bottle ——

⬇ Some families sort their rubbish for recycling.

Some local councils have set up recycling schemes, so people don't have to visit recycling centres. Families may put all items that can be recycled in a separate bin. This is taken away by the council to recycle.

Glass jar

Metal can

⬇ Look out for this symbol. It reminds you to recycle.

As well as recycling, it is good to try to reuse things. Reusing everyday items, such as plastic bags and containers, helps to cut down on waste. Old electrical equipment, such as TV sets, can be repaired and used again.

Building materials, such as tiles, bricks and even doors and windows, are sometimes saved and reused to build new houses.

Where does rubbish go?

Each week, refuse trucks pick up rubbish from our homes and take it to landfills.

Landfills are huge holes in the ground. Refuse trucks tip the rubbish into the hole. Then bulldozers bury the rubbish.

People do not like living near landfills. So some towns burn their waste. They use giant ovens called incinerators.

△ **The trucks tip the waste into landfills.**

△ **Refuse trucks collect your rubbish.**

In many countries, a refuse truck visits once a week to collect waste. The collectors empty dustbins onto the truck, where the rubbish is squashed so more fits in. The full truck then drives to the landfill site.

Many landfill sites are old quarries. The trucks dump their load, then bulldozers pack the rubbish down and cover it with soil to prevent it blowing away. Modern landfills have a plastic liner to stop poisonous chemicals from leaking into the soil.

⬇ **An incinerator burns rubbish to make energy.**

◁ **This golf course was a landfill. A layer of soil covers the rubbish.**

Landfill sites are an easy way to get rid of lots of rubbish, though they are often smelly and look ugly. Once a landfill is full, a thick layer of soil is added. The landfill may then become a park or golf course. It may be hard to see that a landfill was ever there!

Paper, plastic and other rubbish give off heat energy when burned. The heat is used to boil water to produce steam. This steam is used to generate electricity. However, incinerators can create poisonous gases that pollute the air.

Rubbish rotting in landfills gives off a gas called methane. This can be burned as fuel. Pipes set into the landfill draw off the methane gas, which flows along a pipe to a power station.

Does it rot?

Some types of rubbish, such as fruit and vegetable peel, rot away quickly. We say they are biodegradable.

Metals like iron and steel rust. They break into smaller pieces over a long time.

Glass and plastic do not rot. In a landfill, they can stay under the ground for hundreds of years.

◁ Dead animals and plants are food for other living things.

In nature, everything is recycled. Nothing is wasted. Dead plants and animals provide food for living things such as worms, fungi and tiny bacteria.

The nutrients (minerals) in rotting plants and animals return to the soil. Here, they help other plants to grow. We say they fertilise the soil.

⬆ **Manure helps crops to grow but it can pollute (dirty) rivers.**

Many farmers spread animal manure (dung) and plant waste on their fields to fertilise the soil, so their crops grow well. But too much natural waste can cause pollution. If thick, liquid manure, called slurry, gets into ponds and rivers, it can harm water life.

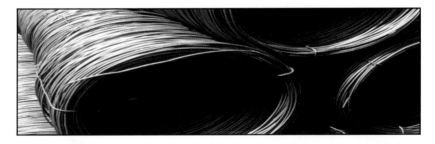

⬆ **Metal wires and plastics do not rot. They can poison the soil.**

Paper, card, cotton, leather and wool are all made from plants or animals. These natural materials rot away. Materials such as metal and plastic do not rot. They remain in a landfill for years and may cause pollution.

⬇ **Look for minibeasts that feed on waste.**

Lift logs and fallen leaves to find the minibeasts that lurk there. Worms, slugs, insects, woodlice and millipedes all feed on plant or animal remains.

These minibeasts help natural waste to decompose (rot). Other minibeasts, such as spiders and centipedes, feed on the decomposers. Always put the log or leaves back gently when you have finished looking at the minibeasts.

Dangerous waste

Rubbish is often solid, like an old can or box. But waste from a power station or factory can also be a liquid or a gas.

Some of this waste is dangerous. It harms nature if people do not clear it up properly.

Cars and homes also produce harmful gases by burning fuel.

△ **Some factories empty liquid waste into rivers.**

⌂ **Power stations produce waste gases.**

Power stations release waste gases as they burn fuels, such as coal, oil and gas, to provide us with electricity. This energy is supplied to our homes, schools and factories to run machines. So, every time we switch on the computer or TV, we are helping to create waste.

When factories make goods such as soap, medicine or paint, they may also produce poisonous chemicals as a waste product. Waste liquids sometimes leak into lakes and rivers, where they harm plants and wildlife such as fish and birds.

⬆**These workers' clothes protect them from toxic (poison) waste.**

Some factories produce toxic waste. This is very dangerous and contains chemicals that are harmful to all living things, including people. Toxic waste cannot be released into the air, soil or water.

Toxic waste and nuclear waste from power stations must be stored in sealed containers. This waste is buried under the ground, but it can still cause problems if it leaks out. It can be harmful for hundreds of years.

Batteries contain metals and acids that can poison the environment. Most batteries usually end up in a hazardous waste landfill. However, they can be recycled. Some towns collect batteries as part of a recycling programme.

One alternative is rechargeable batteries. They can be used many times and can also be recycled when they no longer work.

Throw-away world

Many people are quick to throw things away. They do not reuse things. Reusing means using old things in new ways.

In developing countries, people waste less. They are better at recycling materials. They often repair and reuse old equipment.

When people reuse or recycle, there is less waste. Less waste means less harm to nature.

▷ **This old *freezer* creates waste and can poison the air.**

People in developed countries have money to spend on expensive goods such as cars or computers. We like to buy new things when the old ones break or go out of fashion. All this causes waste and pollution. Scrapped TVs, cookers, fridges and cars may give off chemicals which pollute the natural world.

◁ People reuse the cardboard boxes that this man sells.

In poor communities, people often repair or reuse broken equipment, so less is wasted. Some people sort through rubbish heaps for bottles, tins, plastic, bricks and cardboard that can be sold for recycling. Wood and metal sheets are reused to build shacks.

▽ Some packets have lots of layers!

Next time you visit a supermarket, examine the layers of packaging used on different foods.

Are all the layers really necessary? Individually wrapped foods are fun, but use a lot of extra packaging. They use up valuable materials, such as paper and plastic, which cost money.

△ Packaging can make products look nice but it causes waste.

In the United Kingdom, a lot of our rubbish is packaging. This is the paper, card and cellophane used to wrap products or to keep foods fresh. Colourful packaging also helps to sell products. But when we get home, most of this packaging is just thrown away, which is a waste.

Recycling water

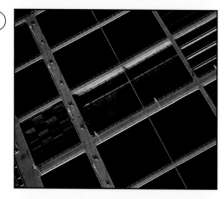

Homes, schools and offices produce dirty water as well as rubbish. Factories and farms also empty waste into rivers. This waste can pollute (dirty) the water.

Waste water from your home goes to a sewage plant. Here, the water is cleaned before it flows back into rivers or the sea. Water treatment works clean the water again before it reaches your home.

◁ **A sewage plant cleans our waste water.**

① Waste water from our homes empties into drains. They carry the water to the sewage treatment plant.

② At the plant the dirty water passes through a grid that removes solid wastes.

③ The water then trickles through filter beds lined with sand and gravel. Tiny living things that feed on harmful bacteria are used to clean the water.

④ Scientists test the water to make sure there are no germs left. Then the water flows back into rivers or the sea.

These children get water from a well. They won't waste it!

You probably turn on a tap to get fresh water. But in dry, desert areas people may walk a long way to get water from the nearest well. They use their water very carefully. The water they wash with is then used to water plants.

Crop sprays can pollute ponds and rivers.

Farmers use water to wet thirsty crops. The left-over water runs back into ponds and streams. Many farmers spray poisons on their crops to kill weeds and insects. When these chemicals drain back into rivers, they can poison wildlife, and people, too.

Save water. Have a shower, not a bath.

Every day, we all use a lot of water for drinking, washing and cooking. All this water has be to cleaned and pumped to our house, which is expensive and uses lots of energy.

Save precious water by taking a shower instead of a bath. Turn the tap off while you brush your teeth or wash the dishes. You can also use rainwater rather than tap water to water the plants.

Recycling glass

Glass is one material that is easy to recycle. Like metal and paper, it is made with raw materials from the natural world.

The more we recycle, the fewer raw materials we need. Recycling materials like glass also saves energy.

▷ **Glass is made in a furnace.**

Glass is made from sand and limestone. These raw materials are mined from the ground and heated in a furnace. They melt to make a hot, runny mixture. This is shaped by being blown or poured into moulds. The red-hot mixture cools to form glass.

▷ **This broken glass is ready to recycle.**

Glass can be made from recycled bottles and jars instead of fresh sand and limestone. The used glass is smashed up to form a substance called cullet. The cullet is then reheated. The furnace does not need to be so hot to melt cullet, so recycling glass saves energy as well as raw materials.

⬡ At a bottle bank we sort glass into different colours.

First, wash your used bottles and remove the lids before you take them to the bottle bank. Most bottle banks have separate holes for brown, clear and green glass, so the glass is sorted before it goes to the recycling plant. As well as bottles, recycled glass can be used to make glass bricks, tiles and fibreglass boats or canoes.

▽ Glass can be reused, so avoid plastic bottles.

Reduce waste by asking your family to buy milk and juice in glass bottles instead of plastic bottles or paper cartons.

Glass milk bottles are returned and refilled up to a dozen times. But plastic and paper cartons are used just once before being thrown away, and plastic bottles do not rot.

Recycling paper

We throw away lots of paper and card each day. But we can recycle this waste to make new books, comics and even banknotes.

When we recycle paper and card, it saves materials and energy. We also help to protect wild forests where animals live.

▷ **These trees will be cut down to make paper.**

Wood is the main raw material used to make card and paper. Most timber used to make paper comes from conifer trees grown on special plantations.
   Wild habitats, such as bogs and heaths, are sometimes cleared to plant these forests. Recycling paper means that fewer timber forests are needed. So, recycling can help to save wild places and the animals that live in them.

▷ **The grey cardboard inside a cereal packet is recycled.**

Newspapers and magazines have lots of ink on them. When they are recycled, it is cheaper not to remove all the inks. That is why recycled cardboard is grey! Clean, white paper is the best paper for recycling. It can be made into writing paper.

▷ Old newspapers can be made into toilet paper.

All sorts of products, including toilet paper and toilet rolls, are now made from recycled paper.

Look out for recycling symbols that show materials have been recycled. We can also avoid wasting paper by reusing envelopes and writing on both sides of paper. Ask your teacher if paper is recycled at your school.

▽ You can also recycle your Christmas tree.

Christmas trees are also grown on conifer plantations. Many councils now provide special recycling points where trees can be left after Christmas.

So, instead of dumping your tree, recycle it! The trees are cut into chips to make a rich compost which can be put on the garden to fertilise the soil.

23

Recycling metal

We make metals by digging up minerals and then heating them in a hot fire or furnace.

Minerals like silver, copper and lead are hard to find. So, people do not usually throw them away. But we do throw away lots and lots of steel and aluminium cans.

Luckily, it is easy to recycle metals, which saves minerals and energy.

▷ **This hot furnace is making iron.**

Iron is a tough metal made by melting iron ore, limestone and coke from coal in a furnace. By adding carbon and other minerals, iron can be made into even tougher steel. Steel is used to build ships, trains, bridges and buildings.

Valuable metals like iron and steel are often recycled. Most steel objects now contain some recycled metal.

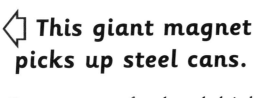

This giant magnet picks up steel cans.

Cans to store food and drink are mostly made from steel or aluminium. At the recycling plant, a large magnet is often used to pick out the steel cans. These are reheated in a furnace to make new products. The steel in your empty drink can could end up in a steel support high on a skyscraper, or as a paper clip!

You can use a magnet to test metals.

A magnet can separate different metals because iron and steel are magnetic, so they stick to the magnet. Aluminium is not magnetic, so it does not stick.

At home, use a magnet to test cans, bottle tops, foil trays and tin foil to find out if they are magnetic. All of these metal items can be recycled.

Mines spoil wild places.

Metals are found underground as ores. When ores are mined, wild places are destroyed and huge piles of waste rock are left behind. By recycling metals we can avoid new mines and reduce waste and pollution.

Recycling plastic and cloth

Plastic is cheap, tough and hard-wearing. No wonder so many things are made of plastic these days!

Plastic does not rot, however. So it often ends up in landfills. There are many different kinds of plastic. Some are hard to recycle.

Cloth is easier to recycle. It can be cut up and put into mattresses.

▽ **These sheets are made from recycled plastic.**

A single bottle may contain several different types of plastic. So, at the recycling plant, plastics are sorted by hand or machine. The plastic is shredded into tiny flakes, which are melted and made into new things.

◁ **Your boots may contain recycled plastic.**

Recycled plastic has many uses. Some is used to make garden chairs, fence posts, waterproof boots or new bottles. Other plastics provide stuffing for pillows and duvets or are made into fleecy coats.

Most supermarkets hand out plastic bags to their customers to carry home their shopping. Because the bags are free, we often just throw them away at home.

Some supermarkets have started charging for the bags. This encourages people to reuse them or to use strong cloth or canvas bags instead. This cuts down on the litter and waste caused by old plastic bags.

△ Old clothes are cut into rags. They can be used for cleaning.

Worn-out clothes and other textiles can also be recycled. You can reuse them as cleaning cloths at home or send them for recycling.

Some old clothes are cut into rags and used to wipe machinery. Other clothes are ripped up and the threads woven to make new clothes or used to stuff seats and mattresses.

Reduce, Reuse, Recycle

You can help to make the world a safer, cleaner place. Just remember to: Reduce, Reuse and Recycle.

Reduce waste by only buying the things you need. Try to reuse items or find new uses for them.

Recycle anything you cannot reuse.

⬆ Buy local foods and reduce packaging.

Reduce rubbish by encouraging your family to buy goods in local markets. Supermarkets often buy their foods from far-away countries. Lots of packaging is needed to protect the goods on the long journey. Foods grown locally often have less packaging, so why not buy them instead.

◁ Reuse pots and containers.

All kinds of boxes, pots and bottles can find new uses at home. Cardboard boxes can be used to store books, toys or CDs. Plastic ice cream tubs can become lunch boxes. Glass bottles and jars can be used to hold pencils or flowers, or you can use them to grow plants. Decorate them with bright paints or stick on pictures from magazines.

⬇ Find out more! These pencils are made from recycled plastic cups.

If you want to find out more about recycling, look at these websites:

- To find your nearest recycling site:
  www.recycle-more.co.uk
  www.wastewise.gov.au

- To find out about recycling schemes:
  www.rethinkrubbish.com/home/

- To look at some recycled goods:
  www.smile-plastics.co.uk
  www.www.cutouts.net

- For lots of facts about recycling:
  www.recyclezone.org.uk
  www.wastewatch.org.uk
  www.ollierecycles.com/aus/

⬆ Recycle old clothes.

Clothes you have grown out of can be taken to a local charity shop. They may be sold to raise money for the charity, or sent to a developing country.

Unwanted books, toys and household items can also be recycled at charity shops. Even old vinyl records can be recycled – they can be melted down and turned into bank cards.

Recycling project

Find out what your family throws away each week by carrying out this project.

Sorting our rubbish is the first stage in the recycling process.

It takes a bit of effort, but if we all recycle, it really will help to clean up Planet Earth.

◁ **1. Divide your rubbish into bags.**

Ask your parents if you can separate the rubbish your family throws away each week. Use separate bags or boxes for metal, glass, plastic, paper and card, food and plant waste, and old clothes. Weigh the bags to find out which are heaviest, and make a chart to show the results.

◁ 2. Start a compost heap.

Almost all of the materials we put in the bin can be useful. Reuse or recycle paper and card, drinks cans, glass, plastic and old clothes. Make a compost heap using old planks and recycle kitchen and plant waste here. They will rot down to make a rich compost for the garden.

△ 3. Weigh the bags again.

See how little waste is left after you have started recycling. Some types of rubbish will have disappeared altogether. Weigh the bags again and record the results. You could contact your local council to find out how to recycle materials such as oil and paint.

GLOSSARY

Bacteria – Tiny living things too small for us to see.

Biodegradable – Made of natural materials which will rot away quite quickly.

Cullet – Smashed glass, used to make new glass.

Decompose – To rot away.

Fuel – A substance that is burned to provide energy.

Furnace – A very hot oven.

Landfill – A large hole in the ground where waste is buried.

Nutrients – The chemicals that plants or animals need to grow.

Ore – A rock or mineral containing metal.

Packaging – The wrappings used to protect goods we buy in shops.

Pollute – To dirty the air, water or land.

Refuse – Rubbish or trash.

Reservoir – A lake made to hold water.

Resources – The raw materials used to make things.

INDEX

Photocredits

Abbreviations: l-left, r-right, b-bottom, t-top, c-centre, m-middle

All photographs supplied by Photodisc except for: Back cover tr, 4-5, 18bl, 21c — Comstock. Back cover bl — Larry Rana/USDA. 1, 5br, 9ml — Alupro: www.alupro.org.uk. 8br, 12br, 17br, 19tr, 23bl, 23br, 25br, 26mr, 27br, 28tr, 29tl, 30bl, 31ml — Jim Pipe. 3br, 20mr — Rexam plc. 4ml — Digital Stock. 7ml, 16tr, 19ml, 25ml — Corel. 11ml, 26bl, 27ml — Corbis. 13tl, 17ml, 21br, 30tr — Ken Hammond/USDA. 13ml — Flat Earth. 13br — Select Pictures. 24br — George Trian/US Navy. 28ml — Bill Tarpenning/USDA. 29 — Remarkable: www.remarkable.co.uk.